yedda morrison

## Acknowledgments

Earlier versions of some of these poems have appeared in the following journals: *Mirage/Periodical, Outlet, The Object Anthology, Kenning, Lyric&, Raddle Moon, Scout, Technologies of Measure,* and as *Shed,* a chapbook from a + bend press. Many thanks to the editors and the communities they help sustain.

And especially thanks to David Buuck, Laura Elrick, and Rodrigo Toscano for their generous reading of this work.

This book is for Stella.

Library of Congress Cataloging-in-Publication Data

Morrison, Yedda Mari.
  Crop / Yedda Morrison.
    p. cm.
  ISBN 0-932716-65-2
  I. Title.
  PS3563.O87492C76 2003
  811'.54--dc21
                              2003011209

Cover photograph by Yedda Morrison

Kelsey St. Press    50 Northgate Avenue, Berkeley, California 94708    510 845-2260    kelseyst.com

Distributed by Small Press Distribution    510 524-1668 or 800 869-7553    spdbooks.org

Publication of this book was made possible in part by a grant from the California Arts Council.

**table of limits**

# The Cherry Pickers

*not a matter of art as such, but a matter of fury directed to conditions beyond art.*
—Mark McMorris

*An employee of a hazardous waste disposal company is seriously injured when she tries to take a sample from a drum of hazardous chemicals owned by an aerospace company. The 55-gallon drum of chemicals stored inside an 85-gallon overpack vigorously blows apart when the employee attempts to open it. My role is to determine the exact cause of the explosion as well as the degree of negligence on the part of the aerospace company.*

*in dark wet*
*pickers stumble*
*Crop waits just ahead*

twists    half body pitch off its ladder        splits into        again it climbs    sloppy gap        through

which it            enters    uniforms safety            the pickers        are not inside it    though under

        *to pick one's own*        push liquored        gaseous            a pitcher of seed glass        sweeps

out slowly    from the refractory    of fruit            twin surveillance            worms inward    gradual

calculate            reaches under    its skirt        jars under bearded key rings        moon beads

peroxide        deep carbonate        blood moves up            the frozen skin fold

        each leg stem translucent        blowpatch        twins drool        on their double

sea horse            glass in a glass bowl        encroachment    double star        helix    cross

over    and then cross back

on diagonal salt plains riotous it-girls assigned to the pump         blow up breast reference

identical ice houses         inflatable bedrooms         *whoosh whoosh*  its affection is

over-inflated         translating as need         its offspring fart gum drops         gingerbread

high-rise balances on low-end real estate         piano keys         peppermint seaboard         double birth in

sugared minefield         *to pick one's own*         wet pit cream         bruised  forward and back

          ticklish leaves elongate         double stem         double stitch         wishbone         star calcium

staining teeth and tongue         dental dam         its four-pronged tear         is seen as such         its twin

burrows further peeling itself of skin all over         though not seen as such         the wet

          unripened pears etc         visual/verbal bypass station         each tissue commissioned vertical speak out lobotomy but no translatable sex referent          what it wanted vs what it got

      on the path to the factory raising lanterns and blow length          citation of cold

episodic      perpetual rift      one

picker counts handfuls      wanting vantage stands on its hands      how many

does it take to carry prop and mount the ladder      orchard at night  recycled

condoms      electric blanket shorting its wires

*zoom*

*zoom*

mechanical

fire

    flies

*zoom*

*zoom*

by day clears low income housing for income housing       did it mention surviving its vinegar twin
image the memorial trace       double blind       object anonymity (she)    constructs its distance
as rubric of consequence       malady allowance       reaches under its skirt       first
born in the first black cavity              flies north       burrows the tallest peak              with an
innate sense of genital desirability              sea ice melts       stranding its predators       multiple meat
packs    bleached visceral palette       hollow hairs attract light to the flesh body       where it enters it
is picked       by day clears an orchard for
the lucrative       blowling       not yet ripe but swollen       excess of water hypodermically  injected
           fig wound       biblical clutch mold       double dipping       frosted stalks       steps gingerly

the tinseled hostless          in lacerated seed packs          silver harried darling its

for weeding and blowing          manage what     implemented pay station    he mass

not male          general defused female violence inviter


singular (specific) object identity          being          identical blow machine          it

surrounds him          endless anonymous capacity for entrance

0

a rash spreads up it        fur and cleavage        coated or cream filled        consummate volition

      fills with suspended articulate fingers        does it mention    nest of charred and hapless

starlings        its briar patch with corresponding rabbits        *to pick one's own*

it-girl with multiple blow up cherries        produced in plastic and        selling in packs of come

alongside it        let it be cared for and        inconsequential  fruitlings dashed against   mirror props

sloppy its oozing        inside where a pipe expelling steam        is not invented by the

leisure of its poem life        rather an ignition of deviance        narrow knife entry pronouncing

      she        divisible non-multiplying violence        inviter    passive  diminished        double throated thigh thrush          *chirrie*

                                          *chirrie*


cross over and then cross back    *she* is the word remaining         or her    as in hers     but she

is not *it* though (entirety)          living ignition deleted as such        she or hers cannot air pipe to a

suitable surface          nor mine          nor x     claims no discernible damage          becoming

another's pie pie          forward and back          is after a fashion          though no longer *it*

double inseam sealing hair bits          pump and its mirror          it and its prop          floats on wire over

blow bins          as if language too had a period of dreaming          fur on which it is suspended

twinned          lip and chamber          bruised though edible          is seen as such          teeth

through tongue     derivative          entities propelling whose products          eats its cherry husk

husk     faster then faster          congealing

it goes with provisionals        plastic cage with functional coin piece                automatically

rises     stands equidistant from its pre-existent divisible hole          it kisses on the lips        all six at

the bottom say     yuck     pulls back its hair          faster then faster          picking its own     prices

per pasty        in the referent it is diminished                to pick one's own

        bucket of wire     *she*     an accretion        hasn't told the lie          nor lived to regret it

is entered          in lieu of systemic advances

        gloves exaggerate hands    it is dark          need of its mouth          a living ignition of

deviance          each bucket and bin          a breathable function          it crosses the vacated lot in

armored car cans          general defused female violence inviter


*zoom*


        *zoom*

available pronoun is     decapitated artistic retrievalbench          inadequate        double blind
object anonymity          stands in its bucket bought        no such citizen but sailor
          if the thighs part it is          a reaction to the dissemination of personal desire        if the
picker climbs through the artist's window    pulling her tail behind her                if its spinal
ignition of deviance fails in the by and by to
road               its perpetual suggestion and so on          double blind object anonymity         speaks
on behalf of               representative and correspondent relationships to service               securing
     the image as dear     spectatorial and consumptive gender props          pelvis indented
          *to pick from*     suggesting variance          did it grasp the content          it came
empty handed     it (she) was handed

when it (he) came     did it come when he came     is questioned as such     its penis enters
the orchard floor     emerges six yards off     hooded articulate eye map
now natural     ingested as such     wood-covered branches organize sound
     accumulate     pigment     stonefruit     cultivar     histories of physical
damage     emerge from pits

     into confiscated fields

arriving at sub lot b, it refuses the nylon zipsuit and puts inside itself one hearty meal. so that when a small girl opens her mouth for the first time it is to receive. what might exit no longer initiates.

assume privilege still grows downward from its swirl. in an effort to get off the page, the hearty meal traveling up. the wheel chair found in the city dump is civic but rolls circular through the bonfire that was a house, not sentimental.

it enters not as the mouth is entered but a measure of equals to alleviate said infant from the flame. so that when a small girl first opens it is to receive. is climbing a teflon branch toward the shape of a rump roast.

please receiver these rotating head jars. cue. she wheels over the bridge. gyrods,* float up forming fatherly function. rods catch at the folds of her second mouth. she rejects what was never hers but to improve upon. cue. it's not a

matter of lopping off breasts to defeat female function in service of specified power, but reinstating an order beyond hierarchies that sum. it's each plastic, visionary hope chest. said choice of vocations is lovely, not it.

*elongated metal tools used in property disputes

law premediated. a mouth is opened in order that it. what it asserts is a silver. more accurately, a silver screen with a large, heavily outlined. is open to receive. audience performing in function

surrounds it with spectacle. if the mouth as an obvious metaphor refuses to chew. all process repeats. cue. if intention exits the mouth, it is in service of what the mouth will receive. cue. taking the glittery jar from the pantry

is also inside it. a 3-inch meanness. cue. genderless vendors push close to the food bins urging their doglets. there is not, nor has there ever been, a genderless sale. again they are fired. rotarians survey. the wealthy can afford to be minimal. cue.

is mapping an ethical framework toward the unadorned pronoun. is a development said to receive. eating what it comes from
before eating
it itself.

yank sweatshirt over head I'm caught zipper wiping sleep half out of eye my eye half out grabbing for finding container in near dark needs washing socks I'm pulling over socks boots and lacing I'm breaking in my hand lace rag might hold hand me together pulling hair from a face tying together boot might hold writing me together but I'm *utilized* so no distance to say it like a figure you reading together not being about me just moving through door into crap darkness boot holding but loose sleep still half eye eye half out not seeing it self but digging it out and teeth all tied up together and useful

# Aerial Motive

*Each factory is a laboratory of human engineering where vital knowledge is waiting to be organized. In this way, the concept that "employees are people" can be stretched to include the realization that they are "persons" too, with freedom of choice, and therefore more likely to join in where they have complete liberty to refuse.*

Service Is My Business, 1948

A Line or Cordon of People Serving as Pickets

The Crop and 3 in front

wrapped in cotton—

born (here) in plastic pumps i've

wrapped dogged

our dirty nails

soil what's wrapped

in cotton

Cerasus vanished city on the Black Sea grew what ancients called Cherries mid-May she's not writing someone else's from outside my own black topsoil rich in humus and lime found in grasslands of central Russia "image becomes explanation" of elevator tower or crane boom mounted on truck platform from which pickers or launchers raise power lines to service the bastard simultaneously wearing a picture hat that is rapidly firing (or i do) "utterances become images" when ordered to face the camera quickly freezing small bright tree of the Rose family for less had he purchased images of people serving as pickets—she's not writing someone else's from outside my own picture writing?

what say you asspants— am i the double entendre doing breaststroke in the company fruit pot

nostalgia blubbering at the freshly plucked trees— keep me here— my option?

the merger is willing to *keep me here* inside the building between bins wrapped green shipped to New

York—"I'm strictly Central Valley" don't envy that (image extends) road as a future etc i *am* the

mouse in plastic heels with the blooded pee hole

i *am* the *in* function of her body

only can

can *in*

so much

hate-able

see that *in* us

see the camera (face it)

freezing

at the end of an era

our own cruddy folds—*in* it

not the lot she'd imaged but

pools under pools

can only *in*

*in* and then *in*

so much


will the ones still identifying as women please stand up

catalytic birdsong floats

       green

       green

       fork lift

```
        layer 1                    layer 2

A       A       A                  B       B

    B       B              A       A       A

A       A       A                  B       B              etc

    B       B              A       A       A

A       A       A                  B       B
```

8 deep = 50lbs/1 box

.21/box  x 20 box = 4.20/hr

#106/ym

calculate the soldier/worker/mouse ratio—

sprawling population of dependencies is

taxable tonnage

are we new tasks for industry


white pumps on the concrete crack

house

                              predawn

                    The Figures cease

but asking—

who cannot tango in practical burlap

might suggest a Shed for true Diplomacy

The Crop and 3 in front

is wrapped in cotton—

dogged

our dirty nails

again, we're bending to it

Stella Mari

*and to this replies…*

Bread is not a
(progressive)
desire
to eat & rest
*forgive me*

She wipes—
bleats in
shadow

sssss

Anonymous egger
in her hen
house hung
(slides under)
nightly
accounted for
nipples

*scraw    scraw*

Can we eat this
ruined
season
apple

Huckster's handcart
re-returning
the dollar diplomacy
*intended*
among us

Whose locked
box in
a food bin
whose lost
(inside the world)
knocks twice
at the towers of
airtight

holds her down
but feeds me

machine vs. hand
matter vs. light

Tongue
revolving
twice turned
toxic dirt
reveals
no well
dug dry
among us

If the sensation of arms is dead arms picking
Weight across a wrist

Small boy in a public restroom floating
Pipes gone dry inside me

                        If arms fill earth's atomic shell, a people thus divided
                           If the boy, a public arm afloat in printed matter

                           Politicizes need after a ruined civic season
                        If in turn you are a public, afloat in dead arms picking


If the conveyer

hands willed over swell & tissue if

Predawn

The Figures cease

find its Fleshy

spot

&

        *fire*

I. x quad

between an iron post and an iron post x buys a certain desirable p/lot buys a certain desirable p/lot on which to build a Factory x plots an evolutionary sequence between the to go and the to go button the Factory contains the reference of letters no more inside (letters/numbers) than there are out (contained) so they (Faculty) the Letters (sequence) are finite economic repeat

night's circular fire marks the first open house. One-Bagger (hired) counts handfuls:

one rubber plant (just six remaining)
one opera hat (with vintage appeal)
one passenger pigeon (strategic/submissive)

pissing over ice she has plastic pee holes (theirs/his) but no matches
bone in her neck hides a reign of Kingship

ink on her
knee hides the
knee bone born
she arrives on a boat
board resigning from Kingship
she will not marry the Sheepherder's cow

*to destroy a Factory so as to win a strike comes from the word for peasant shoe so practice*

II. feminie

*no lift or vanguard but heightened pee holes*

to sails by her vinyl
pinned itinerant
Bride in literate
clothes or roosting in excrement
over cannery windows
Consumption
operatic

III. femme covert

*no essential Rotarian forfeit*

nor a matter of waking in various
media inside a sculpture rotates
slowly mirror suspended from
thin leather straps
outside what is not
a fish flies
backward towards its salted box

IV.  feminie retold

*only under the most primitive production systems*
*might the worker get full value for the Produced*

Factory in pale stockings
cosmetic gas-light
skin over skin
is Allstrap his
Quota props plastic pink
beside paintings of a failed
Kingship four sooty
hoofed hands

V.  aerial motive

she craves the authority of a Public Art project but is covered in skin
fluctuating workroom activities
limbs (Faculty)
his Quota (it)
the finite reasserts a body
(theirs)
two of the ten
survivors

(the lost count boat boards
salty softly bees and pee holes)

*at noon her rubber torso possibly a hand in a dream or elsewhere twitching up in response. excorio the neutralized/naturalized body. how he loved to and on this basis alone he did*

"o"
to be chosen
(the Sheepherder's cow)

VI.  week four: gestation

warehouses whorehouses theater who houses "others"
in brown baggies with appealing Polarized Eye Flaps
twist at the conjugate base
completed the Factory is positioned near or over
*chirrie        chirrie*

VII.  day bed

*A woman is all that a man has lost*
—Etel Adnan

VIII.  day bed

*the wreck compiled of anything*
*constitutes the wreck*

inevitable
surplus of webbed Dolls
of being written
and written of

less
agent less                    less

not a product but a promo
not a promo but a bunion

                        the Factory completed is not a house
if as she said he is
                               but a house full of
                                            Money
"feminized by pleasure"
                    having slept
                              the sleep of the tended
500 years
each soggy leaf
                    and then having slept

                    *if choosing were*

                    to Ascend the stairs in
                    rags and wire

IX.  access

if her birth was recorded
as the first coup of the Great War
thick female ankles turning in male sequence from the painting of a ship

X.  access retold

Open city

if choosing were                    current          c
the dominant impulse of vocational service

                                       fills above a Tower
to *woman* the act of containment

                                                    *thirst*

                              implicit

                                                         repeat

44

# The Tissue Commission

*I happened to be unstrapped that day and, from time to time, I tried to escape, but Asegurada was watchful and I did not want to make violence against a woman for the sake of saving myself.*

—Leonora Carrington

Above the unit, slack in its function, ovipositor bends at a right angle, diving into the junction of the beak, straight down to the root. eggs are emitted for nearly an hour, breast tools blasting.

The neon sign snaps on illuminating the early life of a broiler chicken, breast blisters puffing. dolly, my utility cell closes her mouth. once a scrappy jungle fowl, now edible biomass, skinny legs, and lacy cell life, breasting.

Dolly is the porcelain sheep, an augmented giver, completely in focus. two by two eggs dabbed in a continuous layer at the entrance of the throat. so begins the study of the pregnant uterus, the developmental condition in the man, the porcelain sheep, the giver, the pig.


By writing this I mean not to suggest
intention as a justified total
a mime syndrome
nor that deconstruction had taken our place
had done its work repeatedly, is
a national vocabulary
to begin
maybe it, flat below fingers
had done formidable work, had shaken our place
when was it and now was not so
History active

In laying eggs inside the eye eunice sought no personal glory. the pig placenta and the man placenta served on matching platters. there's some sort of a contingency study. chopping the chewy muscle of the hind limb, she takes the poem back from him. she's not stopping to interpret but stepping quickly over, straining on the hoseable floor.

Push up! push up!

The nervous system (nervous)
alerting organs of special sense
push up!


By writing this I mean not to produce
literature as enough intention
a letter syndrome
nor that hermetics had taken our place
had done its work in theory, is
a national franchise
to begin
as insertion buckle
had done formidable drainage, had taken our place
when was it and now was not so
socially embedded

The broiler chicken, dolly, the man, the cell yard in general, prepare to take a short but grueling trip through the internal architecture of the human jaw. hinges frozen, tongue fused to the tiny back molars no longer an organ of speech. dolly's affection was never meant to be a superficial dissection of the intentional heart. as he comes toward her she is breasting for everything she's worth. get up! snatching back the poem, his legs molded in a kneeling position he presents tradespeople from daily life as workable characters. he strokes the biomachine's stress and boredom. quiets the poem's opinion. we gain frustration tolerance.

Will the animal writers storm the rapid decompression chamber before the chicks explode?
dolly rolls to her back in mud, exposing several hairs around her exit. red and pink beads sewn to her purpose, she has opinion, grunts about it. If functional language is an anti-historical language, she's a violent surplus particle. get up!


By writing this I mean not to paint
art as a romance leaner
an avoidance syndrome
nor that audience had taken our place
had done its work aesthetically, is
a national fragrance
woody
benign below belt loops
had done formidable diddle, had taken our place
when was it and now was not so
eager

The detached muscle meets the masterpiece halfway. the man notes that cutting off the offending part is an essential move in engineering animal writers. one shoots for supersex and reproduction, accessibility and abundance, bigger and fewer. something like the glowing internal anatomy of a 4-inch fetus after deep dissection of its poetry trunk. a meat revival evangelism.

Dolly means, clean this chicken before the mass of young disappear down its throat. her mammalian thorax swelling unsightly. the cage arrives with its blue spermatic cord. the tag no longer legible. in the contemporary meaning of crafts under capitalism the toes swell first. how will we know you?

Day two and the protein supplement chicks are debeaked. chick-pullers drop them into heavy plastic bags like flowering weeds. inside the hen house the nuclei is projected on the eyeball scrota. dolly, my porcelain cell life, is physically crushed. one entrail escapes toward the neon exit, fully reproducible. the man's uterus is presented on a decorative platter. I breast for him. I breast for dolly who *is* a breast, my units reproduced and floating in the even pink vat, wobbly white cups, inverted. for dolly.


By writing this I mean not to frill
desire as realized intention
a justify syndrome
having taken our collective, potential
had done its work topically, is
a surface experiment
a national recliner
maybe it, balls below forceps
had done formidable ditto, had taken our push
when was it and now was not so
vital

how

it          (                    ) is
                         To Enter

bought shiny

Agent in

.  Or

Was for Others

               unmitigated

an

ancient

repetitive

snow

job

How to Make a Sound by Being Struck

diaphanous
or mutilate

How to re-arrange the Service entrance
To throw what once was handed

we are refusing, repeatedly and tiring
        refusing facts of our Composite
        tiring repeatedly

To cough between Sincerities
        inside a FleshWhip
            doggedly

doggedly
insecticide

doggedly
Truncate

riding the inclusion shock wave
doggedly and tiring

how on hands and knees
spraying cause like a barnstorming jet

how 40 acres of Lead Arsenate scatter prompt citizens

supported by a metal rod

       uterine bonsai

       hanging open to the public

       doggedly

       red-cheeked figures blowing into its fabricated center

       a subsidy for growers

                    how used for crop dusting the helicopter
                        returns from the application of sulfur
                            pulls the reds, the whites, the blues

the Blessing of the Blossoms


how blood cells and semen
frothy on the glass
red, white and blue

how we held a special conference just to deal with these few words

Dear Cherry Blossom Queen

we're talking about bodies
hanging open
to the Public

       a seasonal pattern of susceptibility
       the postharvest life of a plum and its picker


how
quick
this, downy
scull drain

bone
binge, empty
but for air

how promoting tourism
being local and photogenic
taking part in air shows

how

bodies

boil

down

to

purpose

how workerspread

in every pertinent direction

like a bloody compass

*rose*

how State prisoners move the tents, set them up and break them down
how larvae drop to the ground to pupate and merge the following season

*how Storm washed*
*five crates of pits*
*to the rugged shores of a new land*
*how orphaned he is*
*choking through side panels*
*an auto evolution*
*creeps in the same small circles*
*a pinned and punctured coil*

how State prisoners move the tents, set them up and break them down
how larvae drop to the ground to pupate and merge the following season

how     a cleaning solvent used for electric appliances
           a critical o-ring (missing)
           a state initiated rent-a-tent
           fields of non functional vaginas


how I am a Swineherd serving Swine and how they turn their snouts up to me
how kisses wet kisses

how we meet the Manager Pilgrim and his Problems sitting naked in the field
how his colonial seeds coming loose across low hills of frothy flowers
how brand new bugs
bursting in his wind

how he returns to his bruise disorder sheets
pirouettes on the private prairie
how his limbs of frothy flowers
seem to strike out on their own

how this work includes fire simulation experiments

begins In The Metal Doorframe

how a handless

sh        she                nonflammable


Suspended

feeds Cadmium and
Acid through the Argon purifier


*been back there?*

*never left.*

Sometimes there's a moment when everything comes together. you're appearing at a growers' convention with the stronger hair inside you, transgenic rice bursting in clouds. you conquer the economy from which it came, is coming to announce us. here here libertylink, stealth fans aflutter. you're a lifescience corporation patenting seeds and chemical input. a single, sweeping Amberwave to drown in

you're fingering backless tops in white saga mink, breathless white backs in them. panting though the panty plumage of a rarefied bird. you're melding seventeenth century with a pocahontas persona whose trademark is an extreme take on ethnic jewelry. you're living on hydroponic nuts and berries

boxed in glasslight a theme of timber cut from paper. you finger spindly allergists until they rise as if suspended. stepping radiant from pixilized topsoil, you are another half of. have been another. or this illumined has always been. in the grace of the bright green wind machine, spitting artificial flowers

or you have been with another, in it, smearing. full of the one who has come before, shoving biotech down
globalized throats, tonguing and radiant

you are the official opening of the forest floor. a miniature christ translating loosely to bacterial soft rot.
floral but never flowery. you conquer the economy from which it came, is coming
to announce us

full of the one who has come and starving through its cheesecloth, chlorines the air transcendent.
you vacate the site of your consummate torso. your face with its real hair beats lightly at the bovine lips.
stronger hair unwinds inside you

pssst… biochemical gets the last word
pssst… undressed you regret me

love rides into town on a mutated pony. love has others in mind. love washes itself in the public pool.
has sores all over. is symbolically red. struggling the flesh bags poorly love says pssst…
i want you 'til the veins pop out
want you and i will

watch from my leaky, heart-shaped window

       love limping under streetlights, spreading its anus

       it shivers

       shits in dry grass at the edge of a freeway

       it gobbles

       erecting a ledger inside the headbank

       it maps man's damp and trampled moon

       it seeks its own deaf ear

       inside you

# Control Tower Intravenous

*any man with a microphone can tell you what he loves the most*
*—The White Stripes*


*The Forest Service stages a predawn raid of an elaborate roadblock*
*at Eagle Creek, using cherry pickers to pull recalcitrant protesters from*
*70-foot high platforms straddling the road. One woman stands on the*
*platform with a noose around her neck, daring them to knock her off.*

extended moments
     of unbraced length   Devastate

     Reveal   complete relative locations of various
        Members

             he
          adjusts his

   Membership with due regard to speed and fabrication

Numbers materialize then exit

through Human walls or windows

     horizontal shear

     to be resisted

     by Connectors in the New Economy

where I might be standing *next to or inside*

a styrofoam Workbench

my contact surface

inaccessible

.

the Shag Rug or Sport Sandal inside each

borrowed house

*shining* compensation for

American Erections

standing *next to or shining inside of*

bright American moments where I might be

an inside supporter of light Machinery

shaft or laser driven *physically*

or Americans *physically* supporting prosthetic or silk flower Production

Americans as a borrowed individual index of

purely *American* efficiencies

*inside or next to* the Sport Sandal

feet bones spread over

available areas of support

dried or lubricated flowers *shining*

inside a white

Industrial

larynx

the qualifying results are the combined shear tensions of allowable working stress

borrowed houses hold

a *governing* Radius of Gyration

a *circulation* of Radical Thought

*collective* Starvation

spacing between *successive* Holes

our own *allowable* Mercy Radius

where I might be standing

*alone or peopled* in

unremarkable

moments of American Inertia


a failure Mechanism

for Manufacturing American

Tolerance

in a Bed or

in a Box


where I might be Developing a taste for

*passable variations* in American households

for *elongated permissible* eye Standards

for the *appropriate glow* of American Channels

for going about one's day with *nonconflictual*

planes of Manhood

where I might be standing without white

regard to the direction of Applied Force

without regard to the direction of Greater Conservatism

displacement generating a secondary moment equal to the resulting

Co-optible Eccentricity

*collectively* ravaged

borrowed houses compile

a total *allowable* moment

standing *next to or shining inside*

those failing to ask *collectively*

which Peripheral Members are not reflected

in the total *American* moment

standing *next to or inside of*

conflictual planes of American Tolerance

*inside* provisions for Stiffers in the New Economy

*inside* bags of expendable Hands

*shining*

or *standing back from*

a blue microwaveable plate

where I might be secreting rotten

American Longing

*one* in a bed of Plastic Bodies

*collectively shining*

where I might be *shining next to or inside of*

Need

*collectively*

fabricating

shear moments of Unremarkable American Inertia

corroborate the sense that it is reasonable to write

California Produce

if we

cannot think. of

do

or haven't

*will*

    *the snake will be sleeping and I'll pick the berry right over its head* she's hurrying, putting shoe to foot, lacing

the other clubbed in a ditch, hurry

they came from a box of smack

deflatable

with a bow smack each

and a part to stick

blow vigorously apart

hurrying, returning to the nippled floor

squat down there suck

*we just worked*

smack

inside the green stalk

stick

inside you

pulling out the

mommy box

beating its

habit of progress burning

our sheltering

trash

*we sleep in a cardboard box*

       sending forth a thick finger

       turdlike, the buds

       repeatedly

       falling through power lines

       an awkward naturalism or natural disaster

       skirt above each head


       in climbing the wax branch the girl *is* above you her vagina for instance is right over your fat
       scull feeling inferior in climbing but onward floating up like a star shovel grabbed onto held
       against hairs flush on it prolonged stooping her pit for instance once dropped and the forward
       bending exposure to feeling inferior when stooping excessive and taking action lit by a
       wee night light flickers down my empty row


       let the dismiss be gender/class/locale

       *I'll chop it to bits*

       the ripping, the sewing for instance

       have been lived in

tell her to crouch down and be a woman with her mouth

tell her to avoid the bottom branches when falling

      fall clear but hit the ground harder

      not scratched but internally bleeding

      a mealy, co-optable

      fruit smack


      the sign said Help Wanted and he was glad to have

      six heads swirling in the sudsy light

            hands the bucket

            lime and limber

            a radiant squirm

            smacking of wing buzz

            returned and reattached

            our body made whole

            now hangs there

when asked I said "nobody."

but I was barely

an optical compression

an elevated entrance

I beat the doll to death inside myself

and I was still hungry

demanding our due

stepping out from

reattaching

blowing vigorously

apart

After the Potluck, wherein each brings and gives unknowingly the item She could least afford, Young Crowd slides downhill, single file, to the Snow Machine. Young Crowd perpetuates the Snow Machine

Constructing a Generator for its running which hangs awkwardly from a Seasonal Ladder. Infighting is Young Crowd's unspoken agreement, managing times of Vision that might otherwise disrupt. The Snow

Machine Maintained it must. At night Minnie sleeps near to it, a Cowbell snuggly about the stronger Ear, that if Minnie angles off to sleep the Bell, She awakens. Now it is Value. Young Crowd slides

Downhill in Historic Anticipation. The Chapter or Century begins as planned. That which is given lays Claim to what is needed. Need becomes abstracted, untouchable. On an Overhead Projector, Female

Versions of Young Crowd in boots for Seasonal Ladders. They are too, also or double. Near or over
Objects placate. M is a Development Officer just in from the Capital. M, entering for the first time,

Fumbles the Mandatory Vitamin Buster. Sprouting just inside the tube-length steel, Cherry
Supplements and Surplus. Young Crowd observes the Toxic Performative Heap. It is Minnie or M who

Removes Her Underthings. Young Crowd makes Motions. Investing in the Body of the Warm One Minnie
Moves closer. Heat Essentializes the body of the Diminished Other. This is the fact of Chapter Two.

Leaking blue frosting on frost, M's Big Machine is ten late. M's Big Machine comes in from a City
Much larger than its Projected Value. To land upright Near the Warm One from the get go is Stellar

Inside this Tissue is Spring's Brief Profit. Inside this Tissue is the crude outline of the Primary letter A. Inside this Post, Price Control aids Progress. Inside this Progress M coordinates Official Purchases.

Minnie pens History as the Making of the Made. Pens History as a Truck that enters blindly. Argues fact both virtual and otherwise. Crosses, rekindles. Citizen M is the Location of Tendencies

Amassing. M's hostless drags, in no particular order for M. M's hostless unleashes Habits from Her Own Twin Revenue. Young Crowd snickers. Hostless straddles the Snow Machine. Hostless leaves Her

Thighs at the scene of the Metal. Six other Knowledges Gun forward. Action is late. Each length of Insistence is surprisingly short. M takes the Wheel and therefore cannot carry it. Minnie leaves Her

Fruit boxed for the Diminished Other. We share this Responsibility because the Hostless refused it. Forgetting the Gears and Signals M straddles the Wheel down the embankment. M does so

Regardless of Her Coin Potential. Open or closed our Tendency is to trail. A path leading from the Snow Machine along the Lake to Seasonal Ladders. Our Tendency, at tree line is that of Needing and

Burning. M accepts the virtual and literal undoing in order to. We but contain, then Sell Her Reservations. Minnie feeds the Value of Her Big Hip buried in Snow. An imprint on the Value of Fruit Producing Hunger.

We catch and throw the Hook because our Tendency is Social.
Minnie will report that Young Crowd Out-Ate the Others. The body of the Warm One

Becomes the Material Investment. Imprint on the Merit of the Big One buried in Snow. Unbeknownst to Mostly the Ice is Timely Tended. We Drain and Burn the Lake after a less Productive Season.

We gather on the Truck though the Truck is what we carry.  We gather on the Truck and then the Truck is what we carry.